THE
1960s

Tim Healey

Franklin Watts

London · New York · Toronto · Sydney

First published in Great Britain in 1988 by
Franklin Watts
12a Golden Square
London W1

First published in the United States by
Franklin Watts Inc.
387 Park Avenue South
New York, N.Y. 10016

First published in Australia by
Franklin Watts Australia
14 Mars Road
Lane Cove
New South Wales 2066

UK ISBN: 0 86313 703 2
AUS ISBN: 0 86415 032 6
US ISBN: 0-531-10551-2
Library of Congress Catalog Card No: 87-51708

Design: Edward Kinsey
Editor: Sue Unstead
Picture Research: Linda Proud, Jan Croot

Photographs:
AP/Wide World Photos
Australian News and Information Bureau
Bull Publishing
Camera Press
Design Council
Hulton Picture Library
Kobal Collection
NASA
Naval Photographic Center
Novosti
Photo Source
Popperfoto
Private Eye
Science Photo Library
Tate Gallery
Topham
United Artists
UPI/Bettmann Newsphotos
Vintage Magazine Company

Printed in Belgium

Contents

Introduction

The 1960s were a time of astonishing developments in science and technology. Not only did people walk for the first time on the Moon; they also looked back and saw our own planet from outside, suspended like a blue oasis in space.

What use was humankind making of the Earth? Terrible violence raged in Vietnam, the Middle East, Africa and elsewhere, and rivalry between groups of countries gave rise to serious fears of a nuclear war. Yet there was also a belief that, with goodwill between nations, science might solve many age-old problems.

World hunger, for example, might be conquered forever by new farming techniques. Disease need not be a problem in a decade that saw the first human heart transplants. Through satellite communication and the new electronic media, people throughout the world were being brought closer together, forming what Canadian writer Marshall McLuhan called a "global village."

The 1960s were, in general, years of hope, when it was possible to imagine an ever more comfortable future. And perhaps that was one reason why young people in many wealthy countries began to question traditional ideas about the need to struggle and compete in society. They wanted more relaxed ways of living founded on the ideas of love, peace – and sheer enjoyment.

People were prepared to experiment, whether with sex, drugs or religion; with new political ideas; and with new musical forms. Fashions became colorful and imaginative. Many boys grew their hair long and wore softer, more feminine styles than before, whereas many girls adopted trousers and a boyish look. By the end of the decade it was often hard to tell the sexes apart.

Not all experiments were successful. Revolutionary politics, for example, never took root in the wealthy nations; abuse of drugs among the young resulted in many personal tragedies. Nevertheless, change was always in the air – in the 1960s it seemed that just about anything was possible.

The United States in the 1960s

Speaking in 1960, the young presidential candidate John F. Kennedy said that the United States stood on the edge of a "New Frontier" of progress and prosperity. And it was true. Throughout the 1960s, commerce boomed and people came to expect ever higher living standards. With prosperity came reform: President Kennedy began to tackle the problems of poverty and racial injustice, and his successor Lyndon B. Johnson continued with a program of his own. It was called the "Great Society": education was reformed, medical insurance set up, and the black's right to vote enforced.

These advances were matched by sensational developments in space technology, climaxing in 1969 with the Moon landing. Yet the country was deeply troubled too. During the 1960s the United States entered the Vietnam war, a conflict which became a national nightmare. At home, violence flared in the struggle for civil rights. And a series of assassinations rocked the country. Among the victims was President Kennedy himself – shot dead in a Dallas motorcade.

△Presidential candidate John F. Kennedy (left) shakes hands with Republican Richard Nixon after one of their TV debates of 1960. The two men opened a new media age by debating campaign issues on TV. Kennedy's better performance in front of the cameras may have won him the election that year.

◁Alan B. Shepard makes final preparations for his historic mission. On May 5, 1961 he made the first American manned spaceflight in *Freedom 7*. Shepard went to a height of 187 km (116 miles), but did not go into orbit. John Glenn made the first American orbital spaceflight the following year.

△Selma, Alabama, March 7, 1965: civil rights campaigner John Lewis cowers as a state trooper swings his club. The episode occurred during an attempted march on the state capitol at Montgomery. Police brutality against demonstrators at Selma troubled consciences nationwide; calls for government action became louder.

▷Anti-war protesters converge on New York. In this early march heading for the United Nations building, 100,000 people demonstrated against American involvement in Vietnam. Among those who addressed the rally was civil rights campaigner Martin Luther King, Jr.

The threat of war

Early in the 1960s, world peace was seriously threatened by rivalry between the two superpowers: the United States in the West and the Soviet Union in the East. Each had its own allies and each had nuclear weapons. If war broke out, the whole planet would be in danger.

In fact no major clash occurred between American and Soviet forces. But there were many tense moments. In May 1960, East-West talks were broken off when an American U-2 spy plane was shot down over Soviet territory. In August 1961, the divided city of Berlin became a flashpoint. The authorities in East Berlin built a wall along the boundary with West Berlin, preventing the free movement of people between East Germany and West Germany.

The worst crisis developed over Cuba. In 1962, it became known that Cuba was the site of missiles imported from the Soviet Union. Because these were capable of hitting cities in North America, the U.S. government demanded their removal. After an anxious period the Soviet Union agreed.

As time passed, tension eased, but the world remained divided. Czechoslovakia (an Eastern bloc country) tried to introduce a more liberal and democratic government; its experiment was crushed by Soviet troops in 1968.

△Gary Powers was the pilot of an American U-2 spy plane. The United States government at first denied its use of spy flights, but admitted to them when it was revealed that the pilot had survived. Powers was tried and imprisoned in Moscow. He was exchanged for a captured Soviet agent in 1962.

◁Fidel Castro was Cuban premier at the time of the missile crisis. He had won power in 1959 by revolutionary means, and soon afterwards declared himself a Communist. In 1961 President Kennedy backed a disastrous attempt to overthrow him.

▷Soviet tanks rumble through the streets of Prague, the Czech capital, in 1968. Five Eastern bloc countries took part in the invasion. Its purpose was to crush the reforming government of Alexander Dubcek. Armed resistance would have been futile, but Czechs demonstrated openly against the tanks.

▽The Berlin Wall, seen from the Western side. The barrier went up almost overnight in August 1961, and it soon claimed victims. The memorial here is to a 23-year-old named Bernd Luenser who died in October 1961 trying to jump across from a tall building.

Assassination

On Friday November 22, 1963, the popular president John F. Kennedy was being driven through Dallas, Texas, in an open car. Suddenly shots were fired. The president slumped; the driver rushed to a hospital, but nothing could be done to save Kennedy's life.

The supposed assassin was a man named Lee Harvey Oswald, who worked at the building from which the shots were fired. Oswald was arrested. But as he was being moved from a police station to the county jail, he was shot and killed by a local nightclub owner.

The Kennedy assassination stunned the world, and Oswald's murder gave rise to suspicions. Had there been a conspiracy to kill the president? Was Oswald silenced? Although an official report concluded that Oswald acted alone, the whole terrible episode left people shaken. And there were more shocks to come. In April 1968, civil rights leader Martin Luther King Jr. was assassinated in Memphis, Tennessee. In June 1968, John F. Kennedy's brother Robert was murdered. It seemed that no public figure was safe from the threat of violent death.

△President Kennedy photographed with his wife Jacqueline and their daughter Caroline. Like all politicians, Kennedy had his critics. Yet he unquestionably brought an air of youthful hope and glamour to the presidency, and these qualities made the assassination seem all the more shocking.

◁Death in Dallas: this blurred photograph is taken from an onlooker's movie film. It records the fatal moments after the shots were fired. Jacqueline Kennedy, in a pink hat and coat, puts an arm around her stricken husband.

△The Oswald murder.
Suspected assassin Lee
Harvey Oswald winces as
Jack Ruby shoots at
point-blank range. Ruby
was a 52-year-old Dallas
nightclub owner, said to
have been a great admirer
of Kennedy. Millions of TV
viewers saw Ruby murder
Oswald.

▷Robert Kennedy, brother
of the slain president, was
a prominent Democratic
Party figure in his own
right. He was a keen
defender of minority rights
and a critic of the
government's Vietnam
policy. In 1968 he
announced his own
candidacy for US president,
but was murdered in Los
Angeles in June of that
year by a Jordanian named
Sirhan Sirhan.

Civil rights

In the early 1960s, conditions were still bad for blacks in the southern United States. Blacks were kept out of universities; they were segregated in movie theaters and on buses; and many were prevented from using their voting rights.

The Civil Rights movement campaigned against such injustices with mass demonstrations. On Freedom rides blacks and whites rode together on buses through the South to defy segregation laws. Civil Rights campaigners believed in peaceful protest, but they often met violence from southern whites. In 1962, for example, James Meredith enrolled as the first black student at the University of Mississippi. It took 3,000 troops to protect him and put down a riot that left two people dead and more than 50 injured.

Two new civil rights bills passed in 1964 and 1965 saw improved conditions in the South, but many blacks complained that they still held inferior positions. They got the worst housing and schooling, and the lowest-paid jobs. From 1965, black riots broke out in many northern cities and a new "Black Power" movement was born. Its young members were prepared to use violence to try to change society.

△Martin Luther King was a Baptist minister who came to head the non-violent civil rights movement. In 1963 he took part in a Washington demonstration of 200,000 people, and made one of the great speeches of the century. "I have a dream," he proclaimed, that the nation would rise up and live out its creed of equality. He was murdered in 1968 by an escaped convict, James Earl Ray.

◁Civil rights campaigners outside the White House in 1965 protest against brutal police actions in Alabama, stronghold of segregationist South.

◁Athlete Lee Evans, flanked by Larry James and Ron Freeman, gives a Black Power salute from the winner's stand at the Mexico Olympics in 1968. Other black medal-winners defied tradition in the same way.

△A National Guardsman patrols Newark, New Jersey, where black riots in 1967 left 26 dead.

▽Another wave of riots followed Martin Luther King Jr.'s murder in 1968, devastating many cities.

The Vietnam war

From 1954, Vietnam was a country divided between Communist North Vietnam and non-Communist South Vietnam. Eventually this triggered the war between them, and by 1963 the Soviet-backed North was sending guerillas into the South to try to overthrow the government. The United States had earlier begun sending troops to help South Vietnam, calling them "military advisers."

The scale of the conflict quickly increased. In 1965 President Johnson ordered bombing raids on the North, and by the end of 1967 almost 500,000 US troops were in Vietnam. The North, meanwhile, was using its own regular troops to fight alongside the guerillas, with equipment that included Soviet fighter planes.

Horrific war pictures flashed around the world, and in the United States anti-war feeling grew. Why should so many young Americans be killed and maimed in this far-off country? What right had the United States to be there? Peace talks opened in Paris in 1968, but the war itself dragged grimly on into the 1970s.

△The crew of an American B-52 bomber pictured before a raid on North Vietnam in 1967. President Johnson halted the bombing raids in October the following year, after peace talks opened in Paris. However, massive bombing resumed in 1971.

◁Hill 875, Dak-To, Vietnam, in November 1967. Much of the ground fighting took place in jungle country like this. It was terrain that suited the Communist guerillas, known as the Vietcong. American troops used devices such as Napalm, a highly inflammable chemical mixture, to try to clear the ground. But in the end not even the most advanced weapons were successful against the Vietcong.

◁Australian troops make an assault landing from a US Chinook helicopter in Vietnam in 1967. The United States was not alone in supporting South Vietnam. Australia had 8,000 troops in Vietnam and New Zealand, South Korea, the Philippines and Thailand also sent military contingents. Their governments all feared the spread of Communism in Southeast Asia.

▷Three small girls hurry past the body of a dead Vietnamese soldier at Nemo, South Vietnam, in 1968. Similar scenes of pain and death filled the world's newspapers and TV screens during the war. In the United States, it became ever harder to argue for continued fighting; all that people could see in Vietnam was suffering.

◁Refugees flee in 1968 from a devastated area of Saigon, the South Vietnamese capital. In January of that year the Communists launched their so-called "Tet offensive." It was a massive attack aimed at 48 towns and bases in the South. Although it failed in the end, it was very damaging.

The restless world

For a long time after World War II, the United States and the Soviet Union dominated world affairs. But in the 1960s, China under Mao Tse-tung began to emerge as a third major force. China was controlled by a Communist government and was hostile to the United States. But from 1960 China also quarreled with the Soviet Union, claiming that it had betrayed Communism.

In 1966 Mao launched a Cultural Revolution, aimed at building a revolutionary society based on complete equality. Many of the old leaders and officials were put on trial, and Mao became a hugely powerful figure. By 1968, however, the Revolution was causing such disruption that it had to be brought to an end.

There were dramas elsewhere. In Africa, Nigeria underwent a bitter civil war. In the Middle East, war flared between Arabs and Israelis. The fighting lasted only six days in 1967, and Israel won a decisive victory – but came no closer to lasting peace.

△Red Guards hold a mass rally in China during the Cultural Revolution. The Red Guards were an organization of Chinese youth. Mao used them to launch an assault on old Chinese traditions. Each Guard can be seen here holding a copy of *The Thoughts of Chairman Mao,* known as the "little red book."

◁Biafran troops in training, in 1968, during Nigeria's civil war. It began in 1967, when the country's eastern region tried to set itself up as an independent state, Biafra. The Nigerian government took up arms, and in the fighting that followed many thousands of Biafra's Ibo people faced suffering and starvation. The war ended with Biafra's defeat in January 1970.

△The desert is littered with
tanks in the aftermath of a
bombing raid in the 1967
Arab-Israeli war.

▷Israel's defense minister
Moshe Dayan speaks with
Palestinian leaders after
the war. The Palestinians
were the original Arab
inhabitants of Israeli
territory. Thousands
became refugees as Israel
expanded, and they turned
more and more to
terrorism to fight the
Israelis.

Independence

In a speech of 1960, Britain's prime minister Harold Macmillan spoke of a "wind of change" blowing through Africa. In fact, it was blowing through the whole world. It was the wind of freedom – the idea that all nations should be free to govern themselves.

Ever since World War II, the idea of great empires had come to seem more unjust and outdated. Gradually European powers granted independence to their former colonies, so that a host of new nations came into being.

Most countries passed peacefully into independence. But there were violent struggles too. Algeria, for example, had to fight for liberation from France in a fierce guerilla war lasting from 1954 to 1962. There was violence in Cyprus and in southern Africa too, where Rhodesia presented a special sort of problem. There, a small number of whites dominated the larger black population. Britain would grant independence only if the whites agreed to share power with the blacks. The white government refused, and in 1965 declared Rhodesia independent without British consent. It was a one-sided, or unilateral, declaration of independence, known as UDI.

▽Massacre at Sharpeville, South Africa, in 1960. South Africa was governed by a ruling group of whites who operated a system of *apartheid* (apartness) for its non-white population. For example, blacks and whites were not allowed to marry, live in the same districts, or even share public benches. At Sharpeville police fired on an anti-apartheid demonstration: 56 Africans died and 162 were injured. The massacre horrified the world, but apartheid remained.

▷Many newly independent nations held jubilant celebrations and issued postage stamps to commemorate the change to self-government. The list of nations made independent in the 1960s includes:
1960 Cameroon, Central African Republic, Chad, Congo (Brazzaville), Congo (now Zaire), Cyprus, Dahomey (now Benin), Gabon, Ivory Coast, Madagascar, Mali, Mauritania, Niger, Nigeria, Senegal, Somalia, Togo, Upper Volta (now Burkina Faso).
1961 Kuwait, Sierra Leone, Tanganyika (which became Tanzania in 1964).
1962 Algeria, Burundi, Jamaica, Rwanda, Trinidad and Tobago, Uganda.
1963 Kenya.
1964 Malawi, Malta, Zambia.
1965 Gambia, Maldive Islands, Singapore, Rhodesia (UDI).
1967 Southern Yemen.
1968 Nauru, Equatorial Guinea.

Youth in revolt

There was a time in the late 1960s when it seemed that the youth of the whole world was in revolt. Opposition to American involvement in Vietnam was a major cause. Throughout the United States, Japan, Australia and Western Europe, students held mass protests in the streets which often turned into ugly clashes with police. Many students started to adopt left-wing ideas about transforming the whole of society.

Some wanted Communism, but not of the old Soviet sort. They wanted a "permanent revolution" which would aim for complete equality, and constantly challenge all forms of authority. Many of the so-called New Left admired Mao's China and supported the Black Power movement in the United States.

The wave of unrest reached its peak in 1968. In Paris that year a student revolt sparked a national strike which nearly toppled the government. In Chicago hundreds of anti-war demonstrators descended on the Democratic Party convention in the same year; youths were brutally beaten by police while millions watched on TV in horrified fascination. Only when the United States finally withdrew from Vietnam (in 1973) did the unrest really die down.

△Ernesto "Che" Guevara was a great hero of New Left students. Born in Argentina, he was a doctor by training and helped Fidel Castro plan his revolutionary campaign in Cuba. After Castro's victory, Guevara held various important positions in Cuba. But he felt that his main duty was to the revolution worldwide. In 1967 Guevara was captured and killed while trying to organize a revolt in Bolivia.

◁ Chicago police wield clubs and tear gas during pitch battles with anti-war protesters. The demonstrators flooded the city during the Democratic National Convention, 1969.

◁French riot police charge students during the Paris troubles of 1968. They began in early May, with students demanding more say in their own affairs. In the student area known as the Latin Quarter, rioters built barricades and fought street battles with police. A general strike was called in support of the students on May 13.The strikes lasted over two weeks and paralyzed the country.

▷ Anti-war demonstrators place flowers in the gun barrels of U. S. national guardsmen. The episode took place in front of the Pentagon building in Washington, headquarters of the American military command. The idea was to try and combat military violence through symbols of love and peace (instead of yet more violence).

◁Student demonstrators wave North Vietnamese flags during the massive Washington rally against the Vietnam war, held on November 15, 1969. This was the biggest of all the American anti-war demonstrations. Some 250,000 protesters marched on the nation's capital.

Pop music

Youth music probably had more impact on society in the 1960s than at any other time in the 20th century. The Beatles were at the center of the storm. They burst on to the scene in 1962 with mod clothes, a new style of haircut and an exciting drum-and-guitars sound.

Screaming fans had been seen before. But the Beatles had wit and intelligence. They influenced a host of other groups and constantly absorbed new ideas into their own music. One key influence on them was the young American Bob Dylan. He had started as a folk singer but developed his own kind of rock-and-roll poetry which opened new possibilities for experiment.

By the late 1960s music and lyrics were becoming highly adventurous. Rock stars performed at vast open-air festivals and were seen by the press as representatives of world youth. People wanted to know their attitudes on topics such as politics, drugs and religion. The pressures were more than many stars could take. The Beatles themselves broke up in 1970, and other musicians started to look back at more direct, uncomplicated styles.

△Pop styles changed dramatically in the 1960s. The Twist (above) was a dance craze of 1961–2.

◁The Beatles (seen here in 1965) were at first presented as the fun-loving "Fab Four," but their artistry grew as time passed. In 1967 they made their famous *Sergeant Pepper* album which explored psychedelic themes partly inspired by drugs.

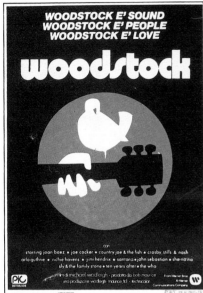

▷ Half a million people attended the biggest rock festival yet seen: a three-day event at Woodstock, New York, in 1969.

▽ Bob Dylan made his name with songs such as *Blowin' in the Wind* (1962). But he later turned to more personal songs of hope and despair, including *Mr. Tambourine Man* (1964).

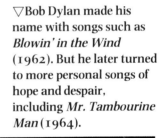

△ In 1969 the Rolling Stones gave a free concert in London's Hyde Park. Motorcycle gang members of the Hell's Angels helped to "police" the event and all went peacefully. The same year, however, a free Rolling Stones concert at Altamont, California, turned into a nightmare when a man in the crowd pulled a gun – and was knifed to death by a group of Hell's Angels. For many people the killing broke Woodstock's romantic spell of love and peace.

Swinging styles

Before the 1960s, most ready-made clothing was sensible, dull – and designed for older people. For men it was hard even to find colored shirts in the stores. Fashions for women were set by expensive designers, and ordinary teenage girls had to adapt ready-made clothes as best they could.

Then came a fashion explosion. In London especially, small clothing shops called boutiques began to open, selling cheap clothes in exciting designs for both young women and young men. The great innovation for girls was the mini-skirt: by 1965 in fashionable King's Road, Chelsea, hemlines were 6 inches above the knee. Bright plastic fabrics, leather boots and false eyelashes all contributed to the 60s look.

For men, styles included velvet trousers, Paisley shirts, wide "kipper" ties and high-collared Regency jackets. Men grew their hair long, too: sometimes to the shoulders or frizzed out wildly for an "Afro" effect. But perhaps the greatest change was that older people as well started to copy the new fashions: youth was triumphant in style.

△Psychedelic patterning on a Carnaby Street shop, photographed in the late 1960s. London's Carnaby Street was made famous by Britain's fashion-conscious teenagers around 1962–3. It was important above all as a center for stylish *male* clothes, almost unobtainable elsewhere. As London's swinging reputation spread, the street attracted hosts of tourists, and became a household name worldwide.

◁Women's fashions seemed at one point to involve ever younger-looking models with ever-thinner figures. The extreme was Cockney model Twiggy (real name Leslie Hornby). At the height of her fame around 1967, she was earning $240 a day as a model.

△The Courreges look of 1965. Courreges was an important French fashion house whose styles showed the influence of Op Art. The white boots, too, are typical of the time.

A hippy couple (above right) dressed in typical "gear" – slang for clothing in the 1960s. "Fab" and "groovy" were terms of approval.

▷ The Beatles dressed in the colourful satin outfits that they wore on the cover of their album *Sergeant Pepper's Lonely Hearts Club Band.*

New values

During the 1960s, many things were permitted which had been frowned on before. The new contraceptive pill, for example, gave women more sexual freedom. People discussed sex more frankly, and nudity became more common in movies and on the stage.

People spoke of a new permissiveness. And the young were constantly pressing to explore their new freedoms. Some experimented with drugs such as marijuana and LSD. Others tried alternative forms of religion, especially the religions of the East.

With their own music, their own fashions and even their own "underground" newspapers, some young people spoke of creating an alternative society. It would be founded on love, peace and freedom. And it would exist outside the harsh worlds of power and ambition which (it was felt) had created the nightmare of Vietnam. "Drop out," was one common phrase. Another was: "Make love, not war."

The movement was especially associated with San Francisco. People there, known as hippies, let their hair grow long and lived in communes, where possessions were freely shared. Their attitudes alarmed older people. And because drug-taking was illegal, hippies often came into conflict with police.

△Hippies came to be known as Flower Children, because flowers symbolized the ideals of love and peace. The summer of 1967 was the summer of so-called Flower Power. Simply to be fashionable even non-hippies decked themselves out in garlands, kaftans, beads and bells.

◁ The Maharishi Mahesh Yogi, a Hindu mystic who found many followers in the West in the 1960s. The Beatles experimented with his techniques of Transcendental Meditation, though John Lennon (seen here) later became very scornful of the Maharishi.

△The interior of a living room designed by Conran and Company in 1966. The effects are typical of the "modern" look of the 1960s. The shapes are simple, the colors bold and the fittings gleam with chrome. Plain pine furniture became fashionable, and the overall style influenced millions of homes through designer Terence Conran's chain of Habitat shops.

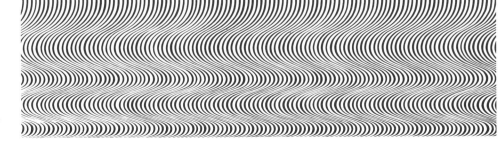

▷ *Fall* (1965) by Bridget Riley, a British artist of the Op Art movement. Op, or optical, art became popular in the early 1960s. It's aim was to dazzle and deceive the eye by using strong geometric shapes, lines and waves.

New in the shops

In the early 1960s, teenage fans played their Beatles records on small portable record players which had only mono sound. Stereo discs were first manufactured in 1958, but they did not become widely available until the mid-1960s. Improved equipment was needed, and by 1969 some fans were listening to their favorite albums on powerful hi-fi systems, perhaps equipped with stereo headphones.

Other new electronic goods included cassette tape recorders, which were first sold in 1963. People delighted in the range of new gadgets (especially the electric toothbrush – first manufactured in 1961). Meanwhile further innovations were quietly changing the "feel" of everyday life. Fiber-tip pens appeared, for example, and people started to furnish their homes with wall posters, instead of hanging framed pictures on walls.

△In the 'affluent' or prosperous 1960s a wealth of inexpensive electrical goods became available to ordinary people. The four girls in this apartment are surrounded by products which include an electric iron, TV, hairdryer, record-player and heated hair curlers.

◁Improved printing techniques helped to make posters a cheap and immensely popular form of decoration for homes. In this collection, psychedelic images of pop stars Dylan, Hendrix and Jagger compete with blow-ups of older movie stars: Humphrey Bogart and Laurel and Hardy.

Me
and my
**Disc
Jockey**

LOOK WHAT I'VE GOT!

It's a Philips Disc Jockey Record Player. Dad gave
it to me for getting my "O" levels. It's *fantabulous!*
It's quite little but it's got bags of volume—*too* much,
Dad says, but you know what Dads are. Disc Jockey
plays all sorts of records—fab for pops or LP's. And
it has a super carrying case you can pop it into
(costs a bit extra—Mum gave me that), with room
for records, so you can take your Disc Jockey simply
everywhere, like parties for instance. The rest of the
gang are *green!* There'll be lots of
heavy hinting in lots of homes between
now and Christmas, I bet!

PHILIPS
—the friend of the family

READ THIS — CUT IT OUT — SEND IT
Philips Electrical Ltd. (Dept. **ABC**), Century Ho
Shaftesbury Ave., London, W.C.2.
Please send me the FREE leaflet describing the Philip
Jockey AG4000, and free voucher for signature on
carrying case.
My name is
Address

If you buy
Jockey
Case (£
you can
ture of D
Eden
Mersey
— free

◁ The Disc Jockey
advertisement dates from
the early 1960s. The text is
clearly aimed at youngsters
who are still at school.
Their increased spending
power came from increas-
ingly prosperous parents.

▷ Dancing to a disc played
on one of the stereo record
players that became
available during the
1960s.

◁ By the end of the 1960s
powerful new sound
systems had arrived. The
picture shows a Rank Bush
Murphy cassette and radio
outfit with stereo speakers.

31

TV and films

In 1965, about 160 million TV sets were in use around the world – five times more than in the mid-1950s. Television had now completely overtaken the movies as the main form of family entertainment. People became seriously concerned that the art of film-making might die out altogether.

Nevertheless, people kept making movies and there were some major successes in cinema. For example, *Dr No* (1962) was the first of the hugely profitable series of James Bond films. And *Easy Rider* (1969) showed that an American film with a "youth" theme, made at low cost, could draw vast audiences all around the world.

Science fiction was becoming popular too. Director Stanley Kubrik made two famous films: *Dr Strangelove* (1963) about the nightmarish threat of nuclear war; and *2001* (1968).

△ Bert and Ernie, two of the animated characters from the junior TV series *Sesame Street.* The first of many hundreds of episodes was launched in 1969.

◁ The Monkees were an American group created in 1966 by some California businessmen to feature in a TV series. It was designed to profit from the Beatles craze, but the four members turned out to be talented and had a series of smash hit records.

▷A poster for *Goldfinger* (1964). With much real-life spying going on between the United States and the Soviet Union, spy stories caught the public imagination in the 1960s. With their mixture of sex, violent action and humor, the James Bond films did well. A critic likened *Goldfinger* to a "comic strip for grown-ups."

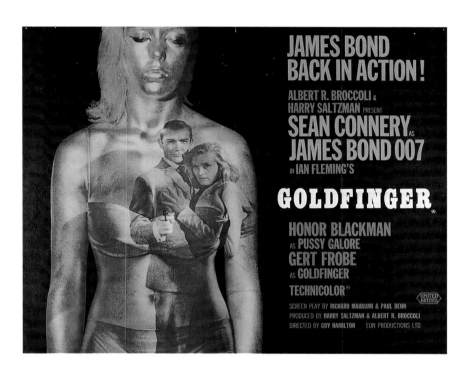

JAMES BOND BACK IN ACTION!

ALBERT R. BROCCOLI & HARRY SALTZMAN PRESENT
SEAN CONNERY AS JAMES BOND 007
IN IAN FLEMING'S

GOLDFINGER

HONOR BLACKMAN AS PUSSY GALORE
GERT FROBE AS GOLDFINGER
TECHNICOLOR®

SCREEN PLAY BY RICHARD MAIBAUM & PAUL DEHN
PRODUCED BY HARRY SALTZMAN & ALBERT R. BROCCOLI
DIRECTED BY GUY HAMILTON   EON PRODUCTIONS LTD

▽A scene from *2001: A Space Odyssey*. Released in 1967, the movie was admired for its brilliant visual effects. It also had a modern theme, reflecting current interest in computers and space travel.

◁*Easy Rider* (1969) described two hippie motorcyclists riding across the United States, who picked up a small-town lawyer on the way. It covered themes of drugs and American violence, and proved to be a surprise hit worldwide.

Sport

For Americans, major sporting achievements were seen in the 1960s. Arnold Palmer won the Masters title three times as well as the British and US Open and Billie-Jean King won three Wimbledon titles (1966–68) in succession.

The figure who most captured world sporting headlines, though, was black American boxer Muhammad Ali. Born Cassius Clay, he changed his name when he became a Black Muslim. The heavyweight champion was more than a great boxer: he also had a showman's flair for publicity. And he became a hero to young black radicals in 1967 through refusing to do military service (which would have involved him in Vietnam). For this he was stripped of his title.

Many other sports enjoyed a widening TV coverage in the 1960s. As a result they attracted more money and became more businesslike. It was at this time that manufacturers started to advertise their brand names on, for example, racing cars. And it was a sign of the times in 1968 when Wimbledon (a tennis competion formerly for amateurs) allowed professional players to compete.

△Long-jumper Bob Beamon was an outstanding American athlete of the 1960s. At the Mexico Olympics in 1968 he jumped an astonishing 8.9 m (29 ft 2½ in), a record that still stood 20 years later.

◁Riding the surf at Hawaii in 1968. Surfing had been a major sport for many years. But in the early 1960s it suddenly became popular among youngsters on the West Coast and in Australia. In California, the Beach Boys created "surf music" with hits which included *Surfin' USA* (1963).

▷Cassius Clay defeats Karl Mildenburger in 1966. Clay was a gold medallist at the 1960 Olympics and went on to become professional world heavyweight champion (1964–7). His dazzling skills were matched by a talent for clowning: "I am the greatest" was his catch phrase. Clay changed his name to Ali shortly before his title was withdrawn in 1967.

▽Billie-Jean King at Wimbledon in 1966. She was the outstanding women's tennis player of the time, winning the Wimbledon ladies singles title three times in succession (1966, 1967 and 1968). Mrs King went on to take the title three times more in the 1970s.

New nations emerged in the arena of world sport. Ethiopian Abebe Bikila (below) twice won an Olympic gold medal for the marathon: at Rome in 1960 and Tokyo in 1964. His country succeeded again when Ethiopian Mamo Wolde took the marathon gold at the Mexico Olympics in 1968.

Transportation

A number of transportation "firsts" were seen in the 1960s. The first vertical take-off aircraft, nuclear-powered merchant ship, hovercraft and high-speed train all became operational. In 1969 the first prototype of the supersonic airliner *Concorde* also made its maiden flight (although regular commercial services did not begin until the 1970s).

All of these were impressive achievements. But for ordinary people the biggest change was the vast increase in car ownership. In the United States by the late 1960s, there was nearly one car for every two people. And although ownership figures were not so high elsewhere, the increases were dramatic. In 1965 there were 13 million cars on British roads – double the 1955 number.

Inevitably traffic jams built up and the need for fast, open roads became obvious. Super highways were constructed, and in the United States the giant Verrazano-Narrows bridge was built across the entrance to New York harbor. Meanwhile, to cope with the special needs of city driving, more families bought a second car.

△Britain's *Harrier* "jump jet" fighter was the world's first fully operational VTOL (vertical take-off and landing) fixed-wing aircraft. Rising straight from the ground, it had no need for long runways – with obvious advantages in warfare. The *Harrier* went into service with the RAF in 1969.

◁The Morris and Austin Mini-minor was the fashionable car for town motoring in Britain. It was created by designer Alec Issigonis and first went on sale in August 1959. The mini was easy to park and quick in traffic. Yet it was big enough for four adults too. Other European manufacturers soon followed with their own mini-style designs.

◁The giant Verrazano-Narrows bridge was opened in November 1964. At that time it was the world's longest suspension bridge, with a single span of 1,298 m (4,260 ft). It stretches across the entrance to New York City harbor, from Staten Island to Brooklyn. By 1969 a second deck had been opened to cope with the huge volume of traffic.

▷ The first high-speed train service opened in Japan in 1964. This was the so-called "bullet train," running between Tokyo and Osaka. Trains went at average speeds of 163 km/h (101 mph).

◁The U.S.S. *Savannah* was the first nuclear-powered merchant ship. It was built on an experimental basis by the American government and began sailing in 1962. At that time few people doubted the future of nuclear fuels.

37

Medicine and science

In December 1967, the South African surgeon Dr Christiaan Barnard performed the world's first heart-transplant operation. Taking the heart from a 25-year-old accident victim, he implanted it in the chest of Louis Washkansky, a patient dying of heart disease. After the 5-hour operation the new heart beat in the patient's body.

Many scientific breakthroughs made news in the 1960s. For example, the contraceptive pill was first available in the United States, and newspapers regularly discussed its effect on young people's sexual habits. In the same year the first laser was made, having an intense beam of pure light capable of cutting through metal. (Laser is short for Light Amplification by Stimulated Emission of Radiation; the first device was developed by Theodore Maiman at research laboratories in California.)

In July 1962 people watched their TV screens as the communications satellite *Telstar 1* relayed the first fuzzy pictures across the Atlantic and made possible instant global news reporting.

With space flight and computers, people were aware of spectacular new technologies. But science was changing lives in quieter ways too, especially in food production. A "Green Revolution" happened in the 1960s. Using new chemicals and strains of seeds, farmers vastly increased their yields of wheat, rice, maize and other produce. Introduced into poor countries, the new agricultural methods often doubled the output of crops.

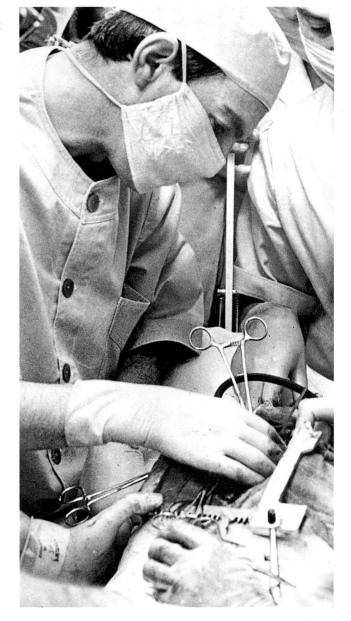

△South African surgeon Christiaan Barnard (above right) did not work alone. In the first heart transplant operation, in Cape Town in 1967, a team of 30 doctors and nurses participated.

◁ The contraceptive pill alters a woman's hormone cycle to halt ovulation – the release of egg cells. After it was made available, women could enjoy sex with less fear of unwanted babies.

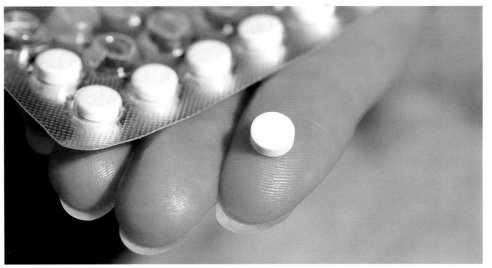

◁Harvesting wheat in the United States. The Green Revolution began in 1961 with the development of a new type of wheat that matured early, gave high yields and could be grown in a wide variety of climates.

▷ *Telstar 1* was the first complex worldwide communications links.

▷Data processing by computer in the 1960s. Computers were becoming more common in industry, but they were bulkier than today's models.

The space race

On April 12, 1961 Soviet cosmonaut Yuri Gagarin became the first human being ever to travel successfully in space. His craft, *Vostok 1*, made one orbit of the Earth and returned to land after some 108 minutes. The flight was a triumph for the Soviet Union, and it surprised many people in the United States. Why was American science lagging behind?

President Kennedy responded in May 1961 by promising to put a man on the Moon by the end of the 1960s. It was an ambitious aim, and Kennedy called for huge sums to be spent on the space program. Some critics doubted whether the goal could be reached, whereas others complained that the money should be used to improve conditions on Earth.

But Kennedy pressed ahead. In 1962 John Glenn followed Gagarin and became the first American in orbit. In March 1965 the Soviet Union's Alexei Leonov made the first space walk; Ed White space-walked for the United States three months later. The gap between Soviet and American science was closing. But who would put the first person on the Moon?

▽ Valentina Tereshkova achieved another "first" for the Soviet Union on June 16, 1963, when she became the first woman in space, aboard the craft *Vostok 6*.

△Soviet cosmonaut Yuri Gagarin was the first man in space. He died in 1968 when a jet aircraft he was testing crashed during a training flight.

◁US astronaut John Glenn enters his craft *Friendship 7* to become the first American in orbit, February 20, 1962.

▷On June 3, 1965 Ed White left *Gemini 4* to "float" for 20 minutes in space, connected to his craft only by the cord seen here.

A man on the Moon

Scientists in the 1960s overcame the problems in getting spacecraft to the Moon. The Soviet *Luna 2* crash-landed on to it as early as 1959; in 1966 the Soviet *Luna 9* touched down softly and sent back TV pictures of the lunar surface. The main difficulty was to land humans – *and to bring them back safely.* That was the achievement of the historic Apollo 11 flight which was launched on July 16, 1969.

On board were three American astronauts. The plan involved a craft in two sections known as modules. While astronaut Michael Collins orbited the Moon in the command module *Columbia*, Neil Armstrong and Edwin Aldrin, Jr. were to land in the lunar module *Eagle*.

The plan worked perfectly. On July 20, Neil Armstrong became the first man to step on to the Moon's surface. He and Aldrin stayed there for more than 20 hours, collecting soil and rock samples. Then they lifted off in *Eagle* to dock with *Columbia*. Millions watched on TV as the three men returned to Earth with a safe splashdown in the Pacific Ocean on July 24.

△Lift-off: Armstrong, Aldrin and Collins are launched from Cape Kennedy on July 16, 1969. Four days later Apollo 11's lunar module touched down on the surface of the Moon. "The Eagle has landed," Aldrin reported to mission control. The astronauts remained in their module for several hours, checking equipment and preparing themselves for the coming drama. Then, on July 19, Neil Armstrong stepped on to the Moon's surface. "That's one small step for man, one giant leap for mankind," he said.

◁Descent: Aldrin followed Armstrong down the ladder some 20 minutes later. A radio and TV audience of many billions of people watched the events.

◁Astronaut "Buzz" Aldrin photographed on the Moon by Neil Armstrong (you can see Armstrong and the lunar module reflected in Aldrin's visor). The two men spent 21 hours 36 minutes on the Moon's surface (2 hours outside the lunar module). They set up equipment and collected samples. They also left a plaque proclaiming: "We came in peace for all mankind."

▽The lunar module *Eagle* rises from the Moon to rejoin the command module *Columbia*. Collins in the command module did not set foot on the Moon. His job involved some anxious waiting. He knew that if something went wrong and *Eagle* failed to rise, he might have to return to Earth without his colleagues.

△Splashdown: on July 24 the command module *Columbia* landed in the Pacific with its crew healthy and intact. However, there were no immediate celebrations. The men had to go into quarantine for 21 days in case they had caught any "space germs."

▷The three astronauts wave from the back of their car as they are driven through New York for a tickertape welcome. In November 1969 three more astronauts made a second successful Moon landing in Apollo 12: Charles Conrad, Alan Bean and Richard Gordon.

43

Personalities of the 1960s

Ali, Muhammad (1942–), born Cassius Marcellus Clay. Black US boxer, world heavyweight champion 1964–7, who was stripped of his title for refusing to serve in the military. Ali twice regained his title, in 1974 and 1978.

Armstrong, Neil (1930–), US astronaut. He took part in the first space docking in *Gemini 8* (1966) and went on to become the first man on the Moon in 1969.

Baez, Joan (1941–), US folk singer, noted as a pacifist.

Barnard, Christiaan (1922–), South African surgeon who performed the first heart-transplant operation in 1967 at the Groote Schuur Hospital, Cape Town.

Beatles British pop group whose members were John Lennon (1940–80), Ringo Starr (1940–), Paul McCartney (1942–) and George Harrison (1943–).

Brezhnev, Leonid (1906–82), Soviet politician who replaced Khrushchev as first secretary of the Communist Party in 1964.

Carmichael, Stokely (1941–), black American civil rights activist. He popularized the slogan "Black Power" while campaigning in Mississippi in 1966.

Carson, Rachel Louise (1907–64), US biologist and science writer. Her book *Silent Spring* (1962) made people more aware of the dangers of pollution from chemicals used in agriculture.

Castro, Fidel (1927–), Cuban revolutionary, head of state from 1959, who established close links in the 1960s between Cuba and the Soviet Union.

Dayan, Moshe (1915–81), Israeli general who became a national hero for leading Israel to victory in the Six Day War of 1967.

De Gaulle, Charles (1890–1970), French soldier and statesman who was president 1958–69.

Douglas-Home, Sir Alec (1903–), British Conservative politician, prime minister 1963–4.

Dubcek, Alexander (1921–), Czech leader who tried to liberalize his country, through "socialism with a human face." He was arrested and made to resign following the Soviet intervention of 1968.

Dylan, Bob (1941–), born Robert Zimmerman. American singer/songwriter whose imaginative lyrics had a key influence on pop music, especially after he used rock rhythms for the album *Highway 61 Revisited* (1965).

Gandhi, Indira (1917–84), Indian politician who became prime minister in 1966 and dominated her country's politics until assassinated in 1984.

Gagarin, Yuri (1934–68), Soviet cosmonaut who became the first man in space in 1961.

Ginsberg, Allen (1926–), American poet who influenced the hippy movement through his interest in Eastern mysticism.

Guevara, Ernesto ("Che") (1928–67), Argentine revolutionary, a hero of the New Left, who was killed by government troops in Bolivia.

Hendrix, Jimi (1942–70), black American rock guitarist whose inventive playing style transformed pop music. His hits included *Purple Haze* (1966).

Ho Chi Minh (1890–1969), born Nguyen That Thanh. Vietnamese Communist who led the independence struggle against the French and was first president of North Vietnam (1954–69).

Johnson, Lyndon Baines (1908–73), US Democratic president 1963–8. His Great Society program extended welfare and aided blacks, but he faced mounting criticism for his policies in Vietnam.

Charles De Gaulle

Indira Ghandi

Nikita Krushchev

Kennedy, John Fitzgerald (1917–63), Democratic president of the United States 1961–3 who supported welfare policies and set up the Peace Corps. His assassination in Dallas shocked the world.

Kennedy, Robert (1925–68), Democratic politician who was Attorney General in the presidency of his brother, John F. Kennedy. A hero of young liberals, Bobby Kennedy was assassinated while campaigning in 1968 for his party's presidential nomination.

Khrushchev, Nikita (1894–1971), Soviet leader 1955–64. He denounced the tyranny of his predecessor, Stalin; broke with Mao's China; and tried to reform the Soviet economy. He was ousted in 1964 after the Cuban missile crisis and the failure of his agricultural policy.

King, Jr., Martin Luther (1929–68), black American churchman and campaigner for civil rights. He preached non-violence and was awarded the Nobel Peace Prize in 1964; however, his assassination sparked a wave of riots.

Leary, Timothy (1920–), US professor who argued that the psychedelic drug LSD could enhance the quality of life by revealing the spiritual dimension. His book *The Politics of Ecstasy* advised "Turn on, tune in, drop out."

Mailer, Norman (1923–), American writer whose books dealt with some of the moral and political problems of the 1960s. They included *The Armies of the Night* (1968), an account of a great anti-Vietnam demonstration in Washington in 1967.

Malcolm X (1925–65), born Malcolm Little. Black US activist who became a Black Muslim and taught that blacks in the Western world should reject white values and create their own society – by violence if necessary. In 1963 he broke with the Black Muslims. He was shot dead in Harlem two years later.

Mao Tse-tung (1893–1976), Chinese Communist leader. As party chairman from 1949 he played a huge part in shaping the new China, and launched the Cultural Revolution of 1966–9.

Nasser, Gamal Abdul (1918–70), Egyptian soldier and statesman who argued for Arab unity and opposed Western influence, forming close links with the Soviet Union.

Nixon, Richard Milhous (1913–), Republican politician in the United States. Defeated by Kennedy in the 1960 election, he returned to serve as president 1969–74, overseeing the eventual American withdrawal from Vietnam. He was forced to resign after the Watergate scandal.

Nkrumah, Kwame (1909–72), first prime minister of Ghana, who helped his country to win independence from Britain in 1957. He became president in 1960, but was ousted and exiled after a coup in 1966.

Quant, Mary (1934–), British fashion designer associated with the mini-skirt look. She opened her first boutique in London.

Smith, Ian (1919–), white Rhodesian prime minister from 1964, who declared UDI the next year. Smith maintained his rebel regime, under pressure from black guerillas and increasingly isolated from the world, until majority rule was agreed in 1980.

Verwoerd, Hendrik (1901–66), South African prime minister 1958–66, who enforced apartheid and took his country out of the Commonwealth. He died by assassination.

Warhol, Andy (1926–87), born Andrew Warhola. American pop artist known especially for his images of everyday packaged goods, and for his silk-screen printing technique. Warhol also made films and produced the avant-garde rock group The Velvet Underground.

Wilson, Harold (1916–), British Labor prime minister 1964–70 and 1974–6.

Mao Tse-tung   Lyndon Baines Johnson

Robert Kennedy

The 1960s year by year

1960

- U-2 spy plane is shot down over Soviet territory, wrecking planned peace talks in Paris. John F. Kennedy is elected president of the United States.
- Independence year for 18 new nations including Cyprus and Nigeria; Harold Macmillan makes his "wind of change" speech about Africa.
- Belgium grants independence to the Congo, resulting in violent disorders.
- Mrs. Bandaranaike in Sri Lanka becomes the world's first woman prime minister.
- China breaks its close ties with the Soviet Union.
- Police kill many demonstrators at Sharpeville, South Africa.
- First contraceptive pills are marketed in the United States. *Lady Chatterley* trial in London opens a new age of permissiveness in publishing.
- Laser is built by Theodore Maiman in the United States.
- Sony develops the first all-transistor portable TV.
- First weather satellite, *Tiros 1*, is launched by the United States.
- Submersible craft *Trieste* descends to the deepest part of the Pacific Ocean.
- Soviet Union successful in the Rome Olympics.

1961

- Berlin Wall is built to prevent East Germans from fleeing to the West.
- Bay of Pigs invasion by Cuban exiles, backed by the US government, ends in disaster.
- South Africa becomes a republic and leaves the Commonwealth.
- India seizes the Portuguese colony of Goa, ending colonial rule there. Patrice Lumumba, deposed prime minister of the Congo, is murdered.
- Independence year for Kuwait, Mongolia, Sierra Leone and Tanganyika.
- Soviet cosmonaut Yuri Gagarin becomes the first man in space. Alan B. Shepard makes the first American manned sub-orbital space flight.

1962

- Cuban missile crisis brings the United States and Soviet Union to the brink of nuclear war; the crisis ends when the Soviets dismantle their missile bases in Cuba.
- Independence year for Algeria, Burundi, Jamaica, Rwanda, Trinidad and Tobago, Uganda.
- Riots erupt as James Meredith becomes the first black student at the University of Mississippi.
- John Glenn becomes the first American to orbit the Earth.
- *Telstar 1*, communications satellite, is launched.
- Nazi war criminal Adolf Eichmann is tried and executed in Israel.
- First public hovercraft service begins in Britain.
- USS *Savannah* enters service as the world's first nuclear-powered merchant ship.
- Beatles first hit, *Love Me Do*, enters the British record charts.
- Brazil wins soccer's World Cup in Chile.

1963

- Nuclear test ban treaty is signed between the United States, Soviet Union and Britain, prohibiting all nuclear tests except those underground (France does not sign).
- Martin Luther King, Jr. addresses a mass civil rights demonstration in Washington, proclaiming "I have a dream . . ."
- President Kennedy is assassinated in Dallas; vice-president Lyndon B. Johnson becomes president.
- South Vietnamese president, Ngo Dinh Diem, is assassinated; American troops in Vietnam number 15,000 by the year's end.
- Independence year for Kenya and Zanzibar (later to form part of Tanzania, with Tanganyika).
- Soviet cosmonaut Valentina Tereshkova becomes the first woman in space.
- First hologram, using lasers, is devised at the University of Michigan.
- First cassette tape recorders are marketed.

1964

- Tonkin Gulf incident results in bigger American military commitment in Vietnam.
- Nikita Khrushchev, Soviet prime minister, is replaced as the head of state by the leadership team of Kosygin and Bhrezhnev.
- Civil Rights Act bans many forms of racial discrimination in the United States.
- Warren Report in the United States concludes that Lee Harvey Oswald was the sole assassin of President Kennedy.
- China acquires the atomic bomb.
- Independence year for Malawi, Malta and Zambia.
- Harold Wilson becomes British prime minister, heading the first Labor government for 13 years.
- Mods and Rockers clash in British seaside towns.
- Verrazano-Narrows bridge is opened in New York.
- Topless swimsuits are designed.
- United States successful in the Tokyo Olympics.

1965

- President Johnson orders bombing of North Vietnam.
- US troops intervene in civil war in the Dominican Republic.

● Black riots in Watts area of Los Angeles last for six days, resulting in 34 deaths.
● President Johnson's "Great Society" opens with the passing of Medicare, the Water Quality Act and the Higher Education Act.
● Black power leader Malcolm X is shot dead in the United States.
● Southern Rhodesia declares UDI under white minority rule.
● Death penalty for murder is abolished in Britain.
● Independence year for Gambia, Maldive Islands and Singapore.
● Soviet cosmonaut Alexei Leonov makes the first space walk.
● Communications satellite *Early Bird* links 300 million TV viewers in nine countries; also transmits the first color program across the Atlantic.
● Japan's bullet train opens between Tokyo and Osaka, with average speeds of over 160 km/h (100 mph).

1966

● Cultural Revolution is launched in China.
● American aircraft bomb Hanoi, North Vietnamese capital.
● President Nkrumah is overthrown in Ghana.
● Indira Gandhi becomes prime minister of India.
● South African prime minister Hendrik Verwoerd is assassinated.
● NOW (National Organization for Women) is formed in the United States, pioneering new feminist solidarity.
● Soviet spacecraft *Luna 9* makes the first soft landing on the Moon.
● Soviet probe *Venera 3* crash-lands on Venus.
● American *Gemini 8* achieves first docking in space, with unmanned Agena rocket.
● Fiber-optic telephone cables are devised.
● England wins soccer's World cup at Wembley.

1967

● Six Day War is fought in the Middle East, resulting in victory for Israel.
● Biafran war begins in Nigeria.
● Argentine revolutionary Che Guevara is killed by government troops in Bolivia.
● New agreements are reached between the United States and the Soviet Union to halt the spread of nuclear weapons.
● Army seizes power in Greece.
● Independence year for Southern Yemen.
● Blacks riot in Detroit, Newark and other North American cities.
● Muhammad Ali's world boxing title is withdrawn following his refusal to do military service.
● Britain devalues the pound.
● Dr. Christiaan Barnard performs the first heart-transplant operation in South Africa.
● Breathalyzer tests for motorists are introduced in Britain.
● Summer of "Flower Power" is celebrated; Beatles bring out their *Sergeant Pepper* album.
● First space disaster occurs when three American astronauts die in a fire while training for an Apollo flight.

1968

● Student riots are widespread: unrest triggers a nationwide strike in France and wrecks the Democratic Party convention in Chicago.
● Tet offensive is mounted in Vietnam.
● Vietnam peace talks open in Paris; United States halts bombing of North Vietnam.
● U.S.S. *Pueblo* is seized by North Koreans; crew is later released.
● Soviet Union and her allies invade Czechoslovakia, overthrowing the liberal regime of Alexander Dubcek.
● Independence year for Nauru and Equatorial Guinea.

● Martin Luther King, Jr. and Robert Kennedy are assassinated in the United States.
● First Palestinian hijack occurs, when terrorists take over an Israeli aircraft flying from Rome to Tel Aviv and force it to go to Algeria.
● Woodstock festival is held in the United States.
● Rock musical *Hair* is first staged.
● Abortion is legalized in Britain.
● United States successful at the Mexico Olympics, some athletes give Black Power salutes from the winners' stand.

1969

● Richard Nixon is inaugurated US president.
● Neil Armstrong, heading the Apollo 11 mission, becomes the first man to set foot on the Moon.
● Anti-Vietnam War demonstrations climax in the United States, with nationwide protests and a march of 250,000 people on Washington DC.
● Skirmishes occur on Soviet-Chinese border.
● Cultural Revolution comes to an end in China.
● British army takes over security in Northern Ireland following increasing disorders.
● Arab terrorists attack an Israeli airliner at Zurich, killing the co-pilot and wounding five passengers.
● Reports of Altamont killing and Charles Manson "hippy" murders in California break the spell of love-and-peace era.
● Supersonic airliner *Concorde* makes its maiden test flight.
● Microprocessor is invented.
● Voting age in Britain is reduced to 18.

Index

12/97   9   8/97